Written by Gaud Morel
Illustrated by René Mettler

Specialist adviser:
Pauline Pears, Advisory Officer,
National Centre for Organic Gardening

ISBN 1 85103 102 2
First published 1990 in the United Kingdom
by Moonlight Publishing Ltd,
36 Stratford Road, London W8
Translated by Sarah Gibson

POCKET • WORLDS

Fruits of the Earth

Think of all the good things
we grow in the garden.

People have always used the leaves, fruits and roots of plants as a source of food. At first, they gathered wild plants and tasted them to see which ones were good to eat. Then gradually, about 5,000 years ago, the first gardeners began to grow the wild plants in plots near their homes: plants like cabbages, turnips, lentils and beans, cucumbers and garlic. Another three thousand years were to pass before carrots found their place in the garden too. As time went by, the wild plants developed into the vegetables we know today. Wild sea-cabbage was the forerunner of cauliflower, Brussels sprouts, broccoli, and green and red cabbage.

◄ Sea-cabbage and wild beet grow on sand-dunes by the sea.

Lamb's lettuce or corn salad

Wild carrot

Wild chicory

As people began to travel further and further away from home, exploring different lands, they brought back vegetables and other plants they had never seen before. The potato must be one of the most common vegetables we eat today, but no one in Europe had heard of it until the middle of the 16th century. **Explorers brought back potatoes, tomatoes and French beans from the New World.** South American Indians had been growing them all for years!

At first, people thought the tomato plant was simply a pretty creeper to grow in the garden. No one thought of eating the red tomatoes till much later. Now it's one of the most widely grown vegetables in the world.

The days of discovering a brand-new type of fruit or vegetable in the wild are probably over, but scientists are working all the time to produce new varieties of well-known plants. They are trying to develop ones which will produce more fruit and be better able to resist disease.

Scientists cross different plants with one another. Seedless clementines and tangerines are a cross between an orange and a mandarin.

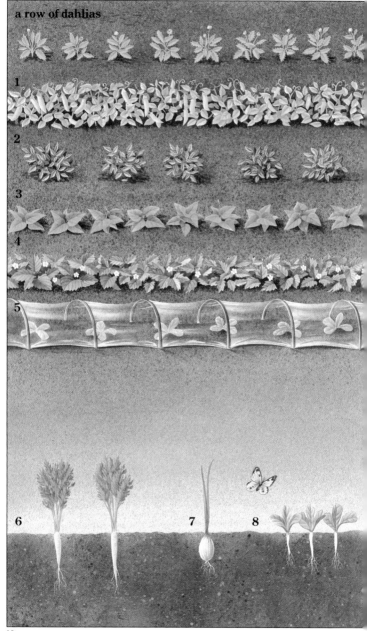

a row of dahlias

1

2

3

4

5

6

7

8

Packet of seeds   A seed potato   Peas in a pod
                 sprouting   and a pea flower

Imagine you are a gardener. **Spring is the
busiest time of the year for you!**
You must sow peas (1), beans (3) and
carrots (6), and plant out potatoes (2) and
onions (7). A potato is a tuber, an
underground store of food which the plant
uses to form its leaves and flowers.
If you want lettuces (5) and
radishes (8) to pick in early
summer, you must protect them
from the cold under a glass frame,
or a tunnel of plastic. Strawberry
plants (4) must be covered by
netting to stop the birds eating
them before you do!

After the last frost you can
move the young tomato
plants from their pots to the
vegetable bed.

11

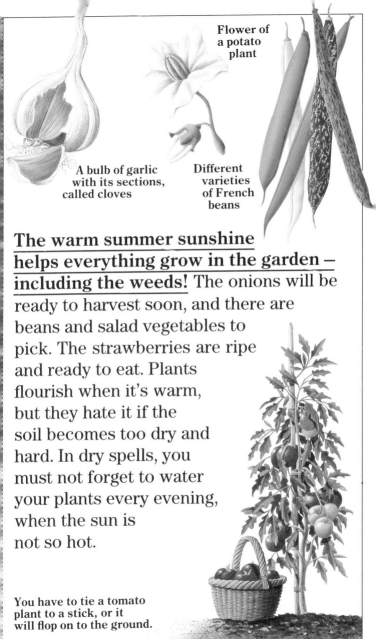

Flower of a potato plant

A bulb of garlic with its sections, called cloves

Different varieties of French beans

The warm summer sunshine helps everything grow in the garden — including the weeds! The onions will be ready to harvest soon, and there are beans and salad vegetables to pick. The strawberries are ripe and ready to eat. Plants flourish when it's warm, but they hate it if the soil becomes too dry and hard. In dry spells, you must not forget to water your plants every evening, when the sun is not so hot.

You have to tie a tomato plant to a stick, or it will flop on to the ground.

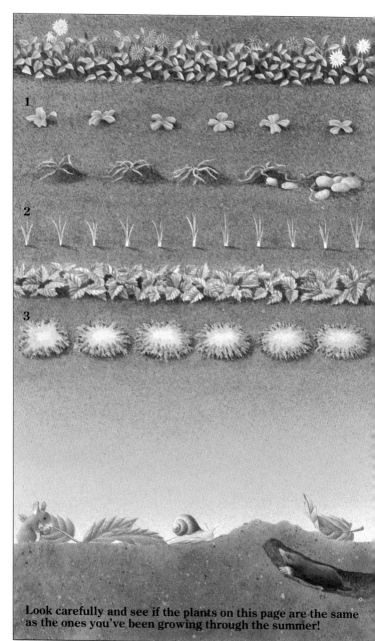

1

2

3

Look carefully and see if the plants on this page are the same as the ones you've been growing through the summer!

Plain lettuce

Curly lettuce

Cos lettuce

It's autumn. The days are growing shorter, the nights are getting colder.

The beans are finished and you have pulled up the plants. Now cabbages (1), leeks (2) and winter salad (3) are growing. It's a good idea to dig some garden compost and well-rotted manure into the soil, to put back some of the nourishment the plants have used up during the year. Did you know that a carrot lives for two years? In the first year, the seed shoots up a bunch of feathery leaves and forms a large orange root, the part we eat. The following year, the plant uses the energy in its root to produce flowers. It scatters its seeds on the surrounding soil, and dies.

Now the tomatoes are ready to pick.

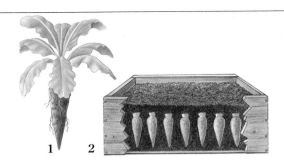

1. Chicory is pulled up from the vegetable bed.
2. Its roots are replanted in a box filled with soil.
3. The root grows a new set of leaves.

In winter, the earth is at rest.

The plants in the garden look lifeless. Many trees lose their leaves so they are better able to fight the cold. Nature seems to have fallen asleep, although birds bring a sign of life to the garden. Now is the time for you to think about preparing for spring planting. Chicory is a slightly bitter vegetable we use in winter salads. When the cold weather comes, its leaves are cut off and the roots are re-planted in a dark box. Without any light, the new leaves that shoot up stay white.

The tomato plant is dead. A new seedling will be planted the following spring.

Globe artichoke in flower

Cauliflower

Brussels sprouts

Can you guess what a kitchen garden is?

Houses with a lot of land sometimes still have one. It's part of the garden which is kept especially for growing fruit and vegetables. Often it has a wall round it with fruit trees climbing up. Do you recognize any of the vegetables on this page? Brussels sprouts are made up of lots of tiny leaves: they are the buds of the plant growing tightly up the stem.

Beetroot is a root vegetable, like a carrot or a radish.

The feathery leaves and pale shoots of asparagus

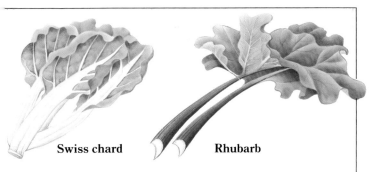

Swiss chard

Rhubarb

Asparagus shoots start to stir under the ground in the spring. The gardener keeps covering them with soil so that they grow into long, tender stems.

Some vegetables are very similar. For example, cucumbers, courgettes and gherkins look alike and grow in the same way, trailing over the soil. They come from the same family as their larger cousins, melons, pumpkins and marrows.

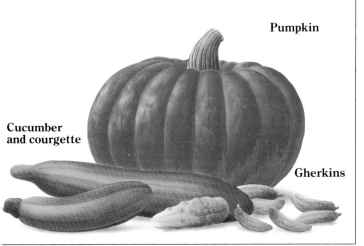

Pumpkin

Cucumber and courgette

Gherkins

The blossom fades, the petals fall, the cherry swells.

Without the help of bees, fruit trees in the orchard would never be able to produce fruit. Let's look at a cherry tree. Bees visit the blossom to fetch nectar, the sweet fluid they use to make honey. Pollen sticks to their legs and backs. As the bees fly from flower to flower, the pollen rubs off on the female parts of the blossom, the pistils, and fertilizes them, so that the flowers can grow into cherries.

Apple   Apricot   Strawberry   Raspberry

Have you ever seen a quince? It looks like a large yellow pear, but it's hard and smells sweet. It is delicious made into jam, or stewed with apples. Medlars are small, brown fruit. You pick them when they are almost over-ripe.

Quince

Medlar

Sweet chestnut

Redcurrants and blackcurrants grow on bushes which are about 1.5 metres high. Raspberry plants grow taller and are usually supported by wires to prevent them from blowing over.

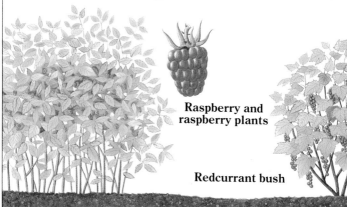

Raspberry and raspberry plants

Redcurrant bush

Blackberry

Mulberry

Mulberries are less common but just as good to eat. Do you pick blackberries along the hedgerows in September?

Walnuts

Hazelnuts

You might also see hazel trees and sweet chestnut trees growing wild in the woods. Have you ever eaten roasted chestnuts? The green husk round a walnut will stain your hands brown if you aren't careful.

Redcurrants and jelly

Blackcurrants and a blackcurrant bush

Grapes grow on a vine which is usually trained along wires so it produces large bunches of good quality fruit.

Plants can get ill just like animals.

Many fruit farmers spray their crops with chemicals to help prevent disease. Can you see the caterpillar inside this apple? It has been there ever since the apple was tiny, feeding on the flesh of the apple as it grew. Greenfly are real pests too. They suck the sap from leaves and stems and make the plant weak and sickly. Luckily a ladybird can eat as many as fifty greenfly every day! The peach leaf below has been attacked by a fungus which has made it blister.

You can train fruit trees into various shapes. Apple and pear trees are sometimes trained to grow flat against a wall.

Herbs give flavour to our cooking. Rub their leaves between your fingers, and they give out a distinctive smell. Thyme, rosemary and bay grow wild in the warm countries round the Mediterranean. There you can see whole fields of lavender, a carpet of sweet-smelling purple. You cannot use lavender for cooking, though. The flowers are dried, and used to fill little bags which you can put in your drawers to make them smell good.

Mint

Sorrel

You can grow parsley, chives and tarragon in a window-box.

A field of lavender ▶

Rosemary

Let's look at some of the fruits which need plenty of sun to help them grow.

Melon plants trail along at ground level. In colder climates they have to be protected by glass frames. There are two kinds of fig, one black and one green. You find packets of dried figs in the shops in winter, but have you ever tasted one when it is fresh and juicy? A kiwi fruit contains as many vitamins as ten lemons!

Black fig

Kiwi fruit

An almond on a tree looks rather like a plum, but you only eat the kernel.

Almond
The nut is the plant's seed.

◀ **Melon**   **Watermelon**

Dates are the fruit of the date-palm. They are full of sugar and very nourishing.

Orange trees need plenty of sunshine and water to grow well. They don't lose their leaves in winter.

Olives grow on small trees which can sometimes live for more than a thousand years!

Other fruit trees grow in hotter climates even further south. **The date-palm was probably one of the very first plants that people took from the wild to grow for its fruit.** Citrus fruits were originally found growing in the warmer parts of Asia.

An orange with its flower, a mandarin, a lemon and a grapefruit. They are all citrus fruit.

They are bursting with vitamins, and very good for us. Their trees are such a pretty shape that they are sometimes grown just for decoration. In colder parts of the world, orange trees are grown in tubs and moved indoors to an orangery, a grand greenhouse, during the winter. Orange blossom is used for making perfume. You can also make a soothing drink from it. Green olives are picked before they ripen, but black olives are harvested when they are juicy and fully ripe. Olives are crushed to produce olive oil, a heavy oil with a rich taste, which we use in cooking.

5 6 7 8
Tools for sowing and planting

1. Spade	5. Trowel
2. Fork	6. Planting fork
3. Rake	7. Dibber
4. Hoe	8. Garden line

Tools for weeding and working the soil

You've dug the beds and raked them evenly. You've sown seeds, and planted out seedlings. You've kept the soil free of weeds, clipped the hedges and pruned the fruit trees. Now comes the moment you have been waiting for. It's time to pick the flowers and vegetables you have grown so carefully!

Tools for pruning and watering

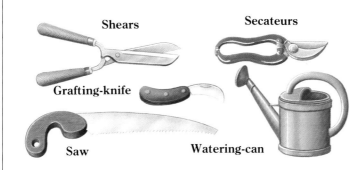

Shears

Secateurs

Grafting-knife

Saw

Watering-can

It's important to know which plants are weeds! Otherwise you might pull up a young radish or marigold by mistake. You have to learn to recognize the difference.

Speedwell　　Stitchwort　　Nettle　　Dandelion

Even weeds are good for something. Once a weed is dead, it will rot down into the soil and help to give it nourishment.

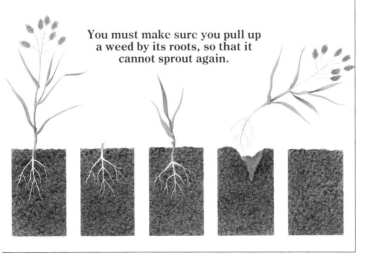

You must make sure you pull up a weed by its roots, so that it cannot sprout again.

Even if you have no garden, you might like to try growing some radishes. You can grow them outside on a windowsill in spring or summer, or indoors all year round. Put a few pebbles in the bottom of a flowerpot and three-quarters fill it with

potting compost. Plant a few radish seeds and cover them lightly with extra compost.

Use a watering-can with a fine
sprinkler to water the seeds,

and put the pot somewhere
where it will get plenty of
light. If you remember to water them every
couple of days, you will have a fine crop of
radishes after about a month.

If you are growing the
long type of radish,
make sure you plant
the seeds deep enough
so that the radishes
don't grow twisted.

Index

apple, 25
asparagus, 18
autumn in the garden, 14-15
bean, 8, 11, 13
bee, 20
beetroot, 18
berry, 11, 20, 22-3
broccoli, 7
Brussels sprout, 7, 18
cabbage, 7, 15
caring for your plants, 32
carrot, 7, 11, 15
cauliflower, 7, 18
chicory, 7, 17

citrus fruit, 9, 30-1
compost and manure, 15
courgette, 19
cross-breeding, 9
cucumber, 19
date, 30-1
diseases and pests, 25
first gardeners, 7-8
fruit tree, 20, 22-3, 25
garlic, 13
globe artichoke, 18
grape, 25
herb, 26-7
hot climates, 26, 29-30

kitchen garden, 18
leek, 15
lettuce, 7, 11, 15
marrow, 19
medlar, 22
melon, 19, 29
new varieties, 9
nut, 22-3, 29
oldest fruit tree, 31
olive, 30-1
onion, 11, 13
orchard, 20
pea, 11
pollenization, 20

potato, 8, 11, 13
pumpkin, 19
quince, 22
radish, 11, 34-5
rhubarb, 19
root, 15, 17
spring in the garden, 11
summer in the garden, 13
tomato, 8-9, 11, 13, 15, 17
tools, 32
tuber, 11
watering, 13, 32, 35
weed, 33
winter in the garden, 17

Pocket Worlds – building up into a child's first encyclopaedia:

The Animal World
Crocodiles and Alligators
All About Pigs
Animals in Winter
Bees, Ants and Termites
Wild Life in Towns
Teeth and Fangs
The Long Life and Gentle Ways
 of the Elephant
Animals Underground
Big Bears and Little Bears
Wolf!
Cows and Their Cousins
Monkeys and Apes
Big Cats and Little Cats
Animal Colours and Patterns
Prehistoric Animals
Animal Architects

Animals on the Move
Wildlife Alert!
The Horse
Whales, Dolphins and Seals

The World We Use
The Story of Paper
From Oil to Plastic
All About Wool
Metals and Their Secrets
What is Glass?
The Wonderful World of Silk

The Natural World
The Air Around Us
The Sunshine Around Us
The Moon and the Stars
 Around Us